SPLIT

First published in 2019 by Blue Diode Press
30 Lochend Road
Leith
Edinburgh EH6 8BS
www.bluediode.co.uk

ISBN: 978-1-9164051-2-7

Typesetting: Rob A. Mackenzie.
text in Minion Pro, 11 pt

Cover art, design and typography: Emily Chappell.

Diode logo design: Sam and Ian Alexander.

Printed and bound by Imprint Digital, Exeter, UK.
https://digital.imprint.co.uk

SPLIT

Juana Adcock

Blue Diode Press
Edinburgh

CONTENTS

their margins, where the wilderness was regaining ground
—Cesare Pavese

for it is with words that we are sustained
—Popol Vuh

The Serpent Dialogues

1

When the woman realised the snake was scared of her too, she went back to the balcony, where she'd at first mistaken him for a spool of brightly-coloured rope. She lay down on the ground and waited, watching as fear took hold of her body: whirlpools of sickness through her limbs, sweat like black ice, her breath sprinting ahead of her and she unable to catch up.[1] She kept wanting to flee, her ears full of fabricated rattle-hiss, but she remembered the way he'd flashed out of sight, back into the encroaching wilderness as soon as she'd taken a step too close. The thought of the snake being afraid somehow helped her stay put till lunch.[2] He did not come back that day, but she decided to repeat the ritual every morning at the same hour. To give him time, even if he needed a thousand years, and allow him to make all the decisions. She lay always in the same spot, on her side, still

---

1   Who were you? Why were you given my name
    since the mountains
    rose up in revolt?
    Why was I given yours with a mouth
    tinged in fire?

2   Even long after my death
    I want my desire
    to coil around your body
    like a snake

as a mountain, her hip pointy as a snowy peak.[3] The snake watched sideways, from a safe distance, and slinked a little closer each day, trying to work out if the woman was a threat. A long time passed before she was able even to unclench her jaw and allow sound to come out. When she finally did, she asked all manner of absurd questions. And the snake, to her surprise, responded.

WOMAN: Snake, what do you think of monotheism? Since everything is holy, I mean

SNAKE: Men – humans – need to organize everything. Messages need to be packaged in a way that's intelligible to them, otherwise they'd be lost

WOMAN: That's why the Mass is didactic in structure, like a theatre play, is what you're saying

SNAKE: Yes, but the sacred element is also built through repetition. Repetition is much loved by men

WOMAN: You don't dislike it either, since you come here to see me every day

SNAKE: It's nice on this rock

WOMAN: There are countless others to choose from

SNAKE: What about you, why are you here every morning?

---

3   Look at this old postcard from Tibet.
    Mountains were taught to us as the picture of stillness.
    But the chaos that went into making that shape
    is still pushing
    up, up

WOMAN: Gives me a good vantage point.[4] I like to look at the valley for hours, trying to understand its contours, the rawness of rocks, their drive. I think you understand this better than anyone. And Snake, did you know scientists still don't fully understand how you are able to move, and at such speed? I looked it up

SNAKE: You have to lean on uneven surfaces, lift up the undulations of your body. To create friction with some parts and flow with others. To gather at your core then shoot out like a slingshot. It feels good

WOMAN: Are you guided purely by your desires, or how do you know where to go?

SNAKE: I follow desire as one follows a thread of light, or a half-remembered song you can't get out of your head. I'm always seeking the next note... Think of desire as an artichoke. Towards the heart, the petals become finer until they're barely as thick as a hair. At the centre there's nothing but a magnetic force, like the eye of a cyclone

WOMAN: Is it something you feel or something you think?

---

4   The balcony a liminal space,
carved from the side of the mountain,
both outside and in. Like what separates
night and day: a purely intuited border.
I thought there were no thorns there, but then I saw
the barbed fences had been sowed into the earth like rows of corn.
Exoskeletoned soldiers on the wealthside,
AK47s at the ready

SNAKE: To me there's no difference. Only men want to leave the body, to define themselves as an intellect in opposition to it, like Descartes.[5] I use my body as a tool for knowledge

WOMAN: You also know how to wind yourself around things, forming many rings around your prey

SNAKE: That's just a practicality. Don't take the analogy too far

WOMAN: Back to the cyclone then. Desire is essentially a creative force, if I understand correctly

SNAKE: Neither creative nor destructive. It's just a force, like gravity. Think how absurd it would be to try to escape those laws

WOMAN: Or to invent a religion that tried to repress gravity. We'd adore a flying woman who never needed to set foot on earth

SNAKE: Don't be silly. Religion was not created to repress desire. It's just there to help guide it and use it, like an ox pulling a cart. The same way we use gravity to operate pendulums, mills, and all sorts of machines

---

5 "*I shall imagine myself as having*
  no arms,
  no legs,
  no body at all," etc.,
  all the memory snatched from the body
  and transcribed
  into books and online:
  how in the process we forgot
  how to learn
  how to know

WOMAN: In that case, what's the meaning of the image of a woman stepping on the head of a snake?

SNAKE: Notice that the woman doesn't call anyone to kill the snake for her. She does it all on her own, with her bare foot. And she doesn't need to think it through. She just does it spontaneously. Why does she choose the head, and not, for example, the neck?

WOMAN: Because that's where the venom is, or to avoid the snake doubling up on itself and biting her

SNAKE: Yes and no. Truth is she chooses the head because that's where the intellect resides. The image speaks to that disconnection I was telling you about

2

Many days went by like this. When at last the snake felt at ease in the woman's company, he ran the length of his body along her waist, cuffed her arm like the sumptuous bracelet of Cleopatra.[6] Lying wrapped in each other, talking, the woman was often surprised at how heavy he was; his weight in contrast with the fluidity of his movements.

WOMAN: Snake, of all the non-human animals in the book of Genesis, you are the only one who speaks. Why?

SNAKE: Because I've been able to make myself into a flute, hollow myself out like a reed and pierce my chest for the right sound, align myself with a divine breath

WOMAN: Divine? I thought you were supposed to represent the devil

SNAKE: All intelligence is in part demonic.[7] Think of the Greek sense of the term *daemon*: it's something you have a

---

6   Let me be a riverbed
    and others the water.
    Let them run through me
    never try to make them stay
    its lights lighting up the path for no one
    ribboning the water

7   Hobbling up the hill like an old crone,
    my head shrouded in dark knowledge,
    I wanted to put space all around you:
    room to breathe
    a night where nothing stirs
    a circle of awareness, expanding
    a train station late at night, its escalators bringing up no one

conversation with. Think about how the whole of civilization oscillates between two numbers. Nowadays we talk about binary language, 0 and 1: all data is composed only of this.[8] In more Cartesian terms, we would speak of 1 and 2, in the sense of complete unity versus separation. That's why you humans have two legs, two arms, form couples and organize your lives always around unity and duality[9]

WOMAN: You have two eyes, too. And a forked tongue

SNAKE: You're right. I guess there's no escaping duality, even for me

---

8   Steve Jobs said the exact same thing:
    the dialogue raced down the screen
    like a river of snakes.
    Wake up, wake up, heart!
    Life is going

9   At this point the familiar call of the train,
    the Canadian Pacific Railway –
    two long, one short, one long –
    wrapped around me
    a child in Monterrey
    beside two tracks in parallel, never meeting

3

At times the snake stood up vertical, his head three foot from the ground, suspended, as if listening for a birdcall on the horizon. Then he would stop answering the woman's questions. In those moments she wanted intensely to reach him, maybe because she knew it was impossible.[10]

---

10 Years later, my lover and I
    invented a word for this: *thalassa:*
    the knowledge that everything will turn to dust
    the knowledge that
        even as we speak
    everything is turning to dust

She thought about how a snake uses a circle differently from how humans do, always outwards from himself, even when going inwards.[11]

---

11 Where did I start?
     The word *I*   like a long thread
     the cloth a weaving of eyes
     (Overheard: "individual freedom is always
     a process of making a world with others.")
     Where did we start?
     By the fire or under a fig tree
     a pinched wisp of combed flax
     licking up moisture.
     The self-propelled twist
     the almost-nothing between index
     and thumb –
     we become still as the weighted
     thread draws circles on its own accord.
     Falling, falling between our fingers
     to the earth.
     This is how a thread is spun.
     As we work we sing with our womenfolk, our men nap or run after
                                                                     deer.
     Babies lie tied to our breast or on their stomach on the grass.
     Where did we start?
     There are no ancient cloth remains, only their depiction on
                                                   eathernware or
     printed on clay like a fossil   the cloth dissipated, the
                                                   thread dissolved
     only the memory of a technique, reinvented
     a history, like thread, erased

And she thought about each time he slid out of sight after their meetings, leaving behind only a brief quiver of leaves.[12] But she was certain he'd be back the next day.

WOMAN: Snake, what do you do the rest of the day, when we're not together?

SNAKE:

---

12 In another language, nothing of what you say
is what you would say. The way of expressing things,
the turns of phrase, *non ancora*
yours.

Yet the moment continues to dissolve
like a butterfly wing between your fingers

4

WOMAN: Snake, when you bite your victim, can you feel its pain?

SNAKE: Sometimes I can, sometimes I can't

WOMAN: Your answers are very non-committal for a snake. What is the moment just before biting like? In film footage we see it happen very quickly

SNAKE: To you it looks fast because it happens spasmodically, like an orgasm. It's not something I have full control over. Sometimes I have blackouts, other times I perceive each small instant with vertiginous clarity. My body tenses up like a bowstring, my head no longer requires any effort to be raised, my jaw opens of its own accord and it's as if my whole being is split into two. I sink my mouth into the soft hair and I feel the warm pulse. As a snake I've renounced the ability to produce my own body heat in order to be able to feel everything, any rumour of blood, any intention to flee. I draw near, invisibly, and deliver the bite in silence. Sometimes I'm not even aware of it until I'm sucking the whole body in. Only when I've managed to blanket-wrap my victim entirely in my skin – and I love being able to do this, to stretch myself in that way – that's when the impulse that I am grows calm, and I sleep with the body inside me. For some time, we are both dead

5

But the snake also had violent mood swings, and the woman suffered immensely for it. Some days he gave her the most fascinating answers, other days he was silent, or sarcastic.[13] That's when the woman started to doubt her own sanity, wondering whether she was the one who was in his space,[14] the balcony not being hers but his, with him being gracious enough to allow her to visit.

---

13 Let go, foot of snow
    melt in hand, melt in sun

14 A fundamental error of attribution
    eggs most fiction on:
    to say "mine," "his," "hers"
    to call ourselves the owners
    as we walk through the forest
    along trails built by the tread of wolves

But even when the snake was in the foulest mood, the woman refused to sever the connection, because she felt their dialogues always taught her something. In this respect, the woman was a formalist.[15]

WOMAN: Snake, what's the true nature of desire?

SNAKE: Everyone asks me that. Don't you have anything more interesting to talk about? That's like asking the moon about the mysteries of love

WOMAN: OK, what's your opinion on Rumi's poem about the mouse and the frog?

---

15 O heartbreak, old friend!
     We preferred to live off the fault lines,
     where the pressure builds and rock is lifted.
     In the shoogling of things.
     In our hermit huts,
     in a place of tension,
     never resting!   I wanted to tell you how much
     our conversations shook up my mind,
     set me forth from my stasis
     into a planetary motion.
     But I could now feel you touch the valley of my neck
     and wrap your fingers around.
     As you gently squeezed, I could see you flirt
     with the idea of strangulation.
     Already feeling the glottis
     close in your grip
     I implored, "Let's live together in a tiny room
     and drive each other crazy. It's what lovers
     do!"

SNAKE: Is that something like the little mermaid? I can't stand stories about princesses

WOMAN: Human-induced climate change and mass extinction of the species. You must have strong opinions on that

SNAKE: Terrible. What else?

WOMAN: What do you do when you can't sleep?

SNAKE: I don't sleep. What else?

6

Then one day the snake didn't show up at all. The woman's mind scrambled for an explanation for what had happened, whether she'd said or done something offensive, whether she'd misunderstood. She called out from her balcony all day long: Snake! Snake!

It occurred to her that it might be some sort of demonstration on his part, a lesson on the structure of desire itself. She cut out a rectangle in the middle of a blank page. She gazed into that window: *look at where desire lives*, she told herself. She made lists of things the snake might be trying to teach her about desire:

1. to create desire you must play with expectation: create a pattern, then break it
2. desire is a friendly embrace that suddenly turns electric
3. desire draws a rosette that starts at the chest and then dances around the whole body
4. desire is also the impulse to run away from what we've done

She thought absence was the snake's method, and she paid attention like a loyal disciple. She began waiting at the balcony two hours earlier than the usual time, observing desire as it swerved around inside her flesh: a rabid monkey thrashing against metal bars. She took note of the shapes, colours, tastes of its rage. She kept a journal, to analyze all its components

Day 19

The sky grumbles like a hungry belly

Day 21

The phone vibrates and I obey,
rising from my chair where I am nestled with a book.
I listen as the sun
draws a rib bone across the sky

I remember an artist who operated on himself
cut open his own chest,
carved out a rib bone,
sewed himself back up,
offered the bone to his mother
for her to use as a necklace,
and she, half guiltily, half glad,
followed suit. What art
can ever be made after this?

Day 22

To befriend my boredom, my wanting.
To notice how it takes hold of me.
How, when I decided otherwise,
and went on a long walk
wearing sandals, despite threats of rain,
I paid attention to this pulse, to the way
the plants shook
and quivered in the wind, as if in perpetual
longing. This longing
also a part
of –

And then
words, mixing lust and tenerezza,
appear unexpected on my screen.

The sky roars, annoyed
at my distractedness.

It seems all I care about is
this impossible encounter, an instant
through the bits and bytes,
up to the stratosphere, through a satellite
then back to earth again:

√√ seen 22:03

Am I really –

All we've
ever
really
wanted
is
to be seen.

To be scene:
watched, contemplated
accepted

Day 23

In the big room, in the church, the place I was so afraid of at night.
I finally come here to work.
To be without internet, to get right down to it.

And I discover the mirror I have been without all these days.
The mirror I never wanted to see myself in. That in the dark I
    was so afraid of.

Switching on the light, those two seconds of terror before the
    tungsten blinks.
The terrible silence of knick knacks, flung.
The broken musical instruments
their tune like the skeleton
of a mouse in formaldehyde.

And I watch as
my brain turns to my phone: wanting wanting wanting

to be

Day 24

In my body, full of scrolling. Scrolls of the dead sea, always
down, down, not reaching. Always eating but never nourished.
Mistaking this hunger for a particular need, rather than a
dis-ease. Before television, we used to sit round the fire and
perform for each other. We still do, but in a way that makes
us feel utterly alone. Our faces lit by the ice blue of a tiny fire-
screen.

I Google this, and the internet says that what I'm feeling is
completely normal. That there are hundreds of thousands of
people like me, scattered around the globe. We tell each other
our most dreadful secrets, this is our way to be home. My
fingers like crabs, moving sideways on the keyboard. I wanted
always to be by your side. It didn't matter to me that you were
a miser, dry kindling, half of your body crushed by heartbreak,
and that you no longer believed in life. I wanted to hook onto
your arm and walk through the streets, heels clapping against
cobblestone, and feel protected.

To instead be one's own wife –

Day 25

I post a selfie

take myself sweetly

to the altar
or the stage

bring myself flowers
and rain

Day 26

I reach for my phone
to check the time
when I can't remember the word
to be entertained
when something hurts, to see what it means
when I can't remember the way
when I know the way but want to make sure
when I don't know the train times
when I know the train times but want to make sure
when the sun is setting, igniting a bridge in the sky
to document this moment
to experience this moment
to experience myself documenting this moment
to document myself experiencing myself documenting a moment
    I'm experiencing
when I'm lonely, to see what others are doing
when I'm uninformed, to see what others are broadcasting
when I can't remember the lyrics, or the tune, to this song
to do my shopping, while at the gym
to open my yoga app, while at work
to arrange a date, while on the toilet

to read an article, while walking from A to B
to check my email, while in the queue at the post office
to see, just to see, if anyone remembered me today
to be annoyed, if someone insists on an earlier message
   I forgot to respond to

my phone to fill in all the gaps

Day 27

To paraphrase the cheesy Charlie Chaplin meme
I saw in a pictureframe on the pizzeria wall today:
silence is gold; we tend to buy noise instead.

And something about reaching for my phone as a form of
noise or interference, like wanting
to be saved from experiencing this instant
with all its beautiful and devastating aloneness

Day 28

The internet tells me that
Hiraeth is Welsh for
"homesickness for a home that you cannot
return to, or that never was"

I am split between this word and its exact opposite:
"a feeling of being at home in the unknown
in which you always are,
and which has always been"

7

Finally, after about a month, the snake came back, breezy as a burn, whistling a song.[16]

WOMAN: Snake! Why didn't you come? I waited for you all day, for weeks, going mad

SNAKE: I fell asleep. I was digesting a mouse

WOMAN: I thought you were trying to teach me a lesson

SNAKE: No, of course not. I can't even imagine what kind of a lesson I would want to teach you, or what for. What are you talking about? Come here, let me hold you

WOMAN: Don't touch me!

SNAKE: What's wrong?

WOMAN: How dare you disappear like that, without a trace?

SNAKE: I've never seen this hostility in you[17]

---

16 Thus the waters were divided,
    their branches
    coursing down the mountains

17 Even long after your death
    I want you lost
    in a silken wilderness
    badly woven
    from my desires.
    I want the reaching
    for my presence
    to turn you to stone.
    Halt this flow

8

The woman watched the snake's head rise, his jaw dropping like a thread of honey, preparing for the bite. They stared fiercely into each other's eyes.

WOMAN: How dare you come back expecting everything to be the same? I felt so ruinous, so – deceived

SNAKE: I'm sorry... the mouse, sleep...

WOMAN: Listen, I know you need to eat[18]. But couldn't you at least send a message? A puff of smoke, a snap of thunder[19]

SNAKE: I did think about it, but it seemed selfish to focus my energies on anything other than digesting the mouse I'd just sacrificed. It's not easy to deprive a being of its life. Since you must do it, because you have no choice, at least show some respect and consideration

---

18 Earlier when I thought of you, the world
    presented me with a dead mouse
    stiff on its side
    in pavement sludge.
    I took this to mean that my impulse
    to take care of you
    to feed you,
    to be around you,
    would lead to a death of some kind

19 *"It is good that you have come, Heart of Sky—*
    you, Huracán, and you as well, Youngest Thunderbolt
    and Sudden Thunderbolt."

WOMAN: What about me? Don't I deserve respect and consideration? Am I not like the mouse?

SNAKE: Our dialogues aren't as violent as that

WOMAN: But we still give and take something away from each other, every time

SNAKE: You're right. Forgive me. You had no way of knowing

9

He looked up, like a puppy at her feet, and drew a figure eight in the sand. A sign of submissiveness and regret.[20]

WOMAN: I thought I'd done something wrong

SNAKE: Forgive me

---

20 Slowly, at the speed at which your fingernails grow
the heat rises from the centre
hits the ridge
is dispersed in two directions.
Slippage and erosion expose
the oldest rock at the top
with fossils of sea creatures

mountains are
an inside
turned out

He said it with such humility that she was not able to reject him. She let him climb up along her arm, steal behind her neck and across her chest. The path left on her skin by his scales ached in different colours. She even let him touch her nipple with his cold nose.[21] When he did, her sex lit up in the dark, like a sparkler inside a walnut.

WOMAN: Can we at least invent something, to help me know where you are?

SNAKE: Whatever you want. We'll find a thread that joins us. We'll tie one end of the thread to my neck and the other to your wrist, that way you'll be able to feel each one of my movements, and you'll always know what state I'm in. Whenever you need me you can just tug a little, and I'll rush straight back. For you, I'll become as long as the longest thread

---

21 At the Villa Borghese museum in Rome
     the painting of Cleopatra by Jacopino del Conte
     is placed directly in front of the light
     so that the sin of a woman nursing a snake
     can only be looked at sideways

11

Here the story bifurcates, like a snake's tongue.

On one side, the woman accepts the snake's proposal, ties the thread to her pinky, and tugs. It works for a while, but then things get rather tangly. The snake gets fed up of undoing knots, of having to remember exactly which way he came to repeat it on the way back. The woman gets tired of always being tied up.

On the other side, there is no knot that can be tied around a snake. This other definition of desire did not even require words to be explained to her.

∽

"In the dress of the girl[...] I see the material it's made of, the work involved in making it[...] As if in a primer on political economy, I see before me the factories and all the different jobs[...] the machines, the workmen, the seamstresses[...] the managers trying to keep calm and the figures set out in the account books, but that's not all: beyond that I see into the domestic lives of all those who spend their working hours in these factories and offices[...] A whole world unfolds before my eyes all because of the regularly irregular dark green edging to a pale green dress worn by the girl in front of me of whom I see only her brown neck."

Fernando Pessoa, *The Book of Disquiet*.
tr. Richard Zenith.

The History of Textile Work Is the History of Civilization Is the History of Desire, Said the Dress

We made an alphabet of threads
word-woven.
My dress said aye, said nay
my dress discerned.

Did you know the words on the tablets of the law
were not engraved but bored
all the way through the stone
so that the letters, made of sunrays
would sear the retina
and print themselves on everything the eye saw?

Did you know that if you looked at the law
long enough
not at the letters but at the slab of stone itself
you could see it billowing in the wind
like silk?

That the law of cloth itself –
that ungraspable essence
upon which empires were built –
was more commanding
than any word?

Il Mago Guarda

I have never understood circles' own
force of expulsion and contention

                              or the weight of the whorl
               or that dusty movement of thumb rubbing index
                         like a magician teaching us to see.[1]

My grandmother more than spinning
appeared to be stretching out
the thread, which wanted to be thread
before it was merely twix and twine

---

1   The magician is a Bangladeshi immigrant
     nicknamed "Guarda" or "Look"
     because it is the only Italian word
     he knows how to say.
     Every night busking in Trastevere
     he asks us to look at
     his white-gloved thumb, index and middle fingers
     twirling the air to produce
     a rope
     that becomes a longer rope
     that becomes a snake
     that becomes a walking stick
     that becomes a rope again
     that becomes a sword.
     Mago Guarda then points it
     at his open mouth,
     head thrown back.
     The crowd, going along with the game,
     screams "*no, mago, non farlo!*"

I cannot tuck the
weft evenly and make a cloth that is fine and will hang over
my shoulders gracefully I have never had
grace but I have desired the way
women are graceful
the way the cloth holds them

hangs from their waist and binds it

the thread falling from her hand like a handful of rice

that she mercifully throws to the birds

searching for the cloth of the Adriatic
or sea silk, woven by women divers who
collect the fibers from the noble pen shells

(it takes 100 dives to gather thirty grams of fibers)

or searching for the transparent shawl held by the Venus of
Cranach

sense of gravity like the arms of saints

or searching for a mythical cloth woven from the saliva of wolves

I have never been able to make
a top spin or to spin on my toes
myself alone

Where did I start?

Silk cocoons in a spiral tree
the silk worm mother

Skirt of Snakes

In the anthropology museum
in Mexico City

the statue
of Coatlicue

wears a skirt of woven snakes
a necklace of human hearts and hands

her breasts heavy from gravidanza
the clasp of her belt a skull.

And where she was decapitated
her spurting blood is two serpents entwined.

Voracious monster mother
loving Earth mother

   tomb /
womb, etc.

She rises at dawn to sweep away the bones
make space for the new

her son
fathered by a feather

is born
fully grown

armoured
for battle.

We, his snake sisters
weave

Juárez / Ecatepec

We were taken down to the river, all eleven girls.
We had stopped being useful for one thing.
A man took a poor view
on what one of us had said.
Or on the fact that some of us had gone AWOL to eat gorditas
when we'd promised to diet during the day.
A man had the theory that we
throated better when hungry.
With that kind of hunger that pulls you down
into yourself, your thoughts clinging
to your ribs, vacuum-packed,
and words are emptied out of you,
and you live second to second like an animal.

In any case, the janitor
led us there on foot.
Hands tied.
Tape on mouth.
Bound to each other by the waist,
a necklace of girls.
He was sent because the job was considered
not worth the while of an expert executioner.
We had to watch as one by one he
hit us in the face with a stone until we stopped moving.
Tied by the waist to the girl to our left; the rope
pulling our middle, stomach tied tight.
Off jaw, out teeth. Nose,
eyes, and between the eyes.
We watched. Right until our eyeballs
rolled back into their sockets
and we gazed into the night of ourselves.
The last of us had already asphyxiated when it got to her turn;

vomit behind duct tape,
burn through the nose
swallowed back down.

Then he left us to feed
the wild boar and the coyotes.

Two years later we were found,
bones dispersed, sunned.
All marked
by the same –

How much machinery
to make that dress, to raise
and put down
that stone?

§

I was looking, in vain, for the newspaper article
that told our story among the deluge of pages

on the thousands of women of similar fates.
At the graves we

summon up our dead
ask them for strength

chant as we gather the remains
clink clank xylophoned in our zurrón

each bone a different timbre
for our song.

We blow on their bones.
With our breath

we build
an army

§

I go round calling out for our
bodies in the house
of the dead:

Wake up grandmother
wake up grandfather
wake up 43
wake up 49
wake up 22
wake up 72
wake up 193
wake up 45
wake up 332
wake up 16
wake up 52
wake up 55
wake up 400
wake up 300
wake up 300
wake up 18
wake up 17
wake up 68
wake up 70
wake up 23
wake up 20
wake up 120

wake up
landless workers burned alive
gamblers burned in the casino
children burned in the day center
the witches burned

wake up
men hacked to pieces
women tortured
migrants suffocated in lorries
lying on the bed of the Seabetween
North, South, East

wake up extinct beasts
forgotten birdsong
torn mountains
quarried stones
corals lost

Stand before us now.
Lend us your voice.

Too long we have walked on our knees
our blood a path
of cempazúchitl petals.

Let us be a bridge.
A bridge

Doors Which, When Opened Inwards, Sting

Glorious the joy of closing one's eyes and seeing someone
close their eyes

Their forearm feeling the drops and just
before asking what's up their throat goes to pieces on the floor

And glorious the key that opened all doors, the one that
a humble cloth we braided like hands in prayer the knuckles
trembling knots crossed into bundles, into footfall
do you want to untie all my knots? unlock all my doors?
        yes, I want to open the doors in your foot: kiss, the
doors in your big toe: kiss, the doors in your astragalus: kiss,
the doors in your soleus: kiss, the doors in your sartorius:
kiss, the doors in your pectineus: kiss, the doors in your
hypochondrium: kiss, the doors in your ventral aspect: kiss,
the doors in your occiput: kiss, the doors in your nuchal
plane: kiss, the doors in your medial: kiss, the doors in your
hallucis brevis: kiss, the doors in your vagus: kiss, the doors
in your subclavian: kiss, the doors in your transverse process:
kiss, the doors in your duodenojejunal junction, etcetera.

Yesterday I caught sight of the shattered haws mid-air
the salty sites we wandered entreating each other
the gaps unanchored, uprooted
the slight song that in the morning rose us

that mother I don't have, the roe
behind my neck where the row is the roe is the row is the roe
    that gestates
the beginning the water where is born that blood that thickens
    disperses ties us down

The naked truth is: this wasp sting is my only belonging; this
    water that heaps up behind the doors in my face

Flood Prayer

Here, me, myself.

My hand, of the five guardians
and a single spillway

says: You are not needed here
says: Here the stone and the woods are drunken
says: There they cry out for you in the blazing plains
says: There they seek out your jade skirt

Our mop of people
our hands the colour of prickly pears

say: There the wind beaten in nine places
say: There you will bathe, there you will cleanse
the one born in your hand
the one who lived in your hand

Not tomorrow. Not the day after tomorrow.
Here, now.

Loosen your fists and let go of earth trees roots pylons
palm tree highrise slippage bent cars
Loosen your fists and drop elevators satellites glass pools clay
    waves down the incline
the colours of cortex we never saw below
electrified saturations dragged dogs waterlogged burnt hair
offshoots of earth tidal
pánuco tamesí xigüe guayalejo undone in refuges

It rains, our faces turn into boats
our boots into barro mudslide
encharcadas

Chubasco chabacano parra tecladeando cumbiamba
desgarrar alter niesto nunca oscura fuga de

Italian Tourist Bureau Draws Up Plan for the Regeneration of the Cinque Terra Landscape

I am land –
cut into terraces my earth
hugged together by roots my water
inking through gaps my stones
holding together neatly my walls
tidy in vineyards and olive groves.

Contadino, you made me beautiful.
From afar

I was paradise. From up close
I was back-breaking work.
From the golden mean I was indifferent
market stalls.
Imports and exports.

Contadino, my love. You left me
for the city.
My stonewalls crumbled
my wild boar stamping
my maritime pines invading
with their high tops and bare masts
swooping in the wind.

My legs were too prickly
for your taste, O contadino.

You were ridiculed for your dialect of scrub.
You ironed it out like a shirt.

Your clean fingernails tapped at the keyboard
in air conditioned rooms
atop staircases made of marble carved out
from my sisters' mountains.

And me, abandoned, returning to my wild state
shaking off your cuttings and divisions
with a few landslides and storms
to wipe my slate clean.

And as the dinghies sink
and those fleeing from war drown
wordlessly in my picturesque sea

the functionaries hold long meetings
at the Tourism Bureau
puzzling over how to reignite
my Contadino's love for me –

they know I am worth more
as a terraced olive grove.

We don't have enough hands
for all the things we need
to hold onto

Letter, 1942

Oh, if we could go back!
Walk up that steep little lane.

It should be a mass of primrose now
and violets
war or no war

The Poet Attempts to Build a House

Carve one brick
to perfection
my word my word

embers at the pit
of my belly

I blow slow smoke
to cool off
the spill
hardening to rock

I carve and
cart the words to
my plot

my legs like a compass
measure out the land

where I must flatten grassblades
dig out pits

an economy of guilt

§

Name the house where guilt lives
comfortable
in my skin-words
a layer under which to hide
or reveal

to adventure on like the Greek
to live in words
to build a house with words
to be writ in stone or sand or snow or water
to spindle your way through
the weft
meticulously
never missing one beat
to make a nest in music,
always immaterial
to nibble your way through a 3/2 rhythm

Steller's Use of Verbs When Describing the Sea Cow, Hunted to Extinction within 27 Years of its Discovery by Europeans. *De Bestiis Marinis, 1751.*

captured / resisting / put to uses / detached / masticates / lies prone / grows / increases / grows / grow / take the place / masticates / move as do the lips of cattle / tear off / cut / cut / softened by boiling / cut like a checkerboard / boiled / yield / may be moved / can be moved / to move / masticate

set in the palate / expressed by no known name / cannot call it / is inserted / are perforated / are inserted / excavated / fit into / will explain / stretch back / perforated / grows / take the place / takes the place / cut / grows / grows / excavated / extend downward like a bow / make a double hollow / grows / is frayed out / ends / is inserted / it agrees / with an up-and-down motion drives itself violently forward / struggles to escape / this happened by mere chance

walks as with feet / fights / resists / swimming prone / embraces / holds and permits herself in turn to be embraced / are exactly as man / have not yet given birth / is not swollen / to get the milk in large quantities from dead ones in the same way as from cows / cut / give out milk / collected by squeezing / boiled / reaches clear to / ends / enter / cut / cut / were not found / were found / given this round form / seen / is inserted / move / to happen / was done / was perforated / had penetrated / cut / took / thought / cut / saw / it happened / cut / had been hired / took the place of money / became tired / inspect / make tessellated like a checkerboard / present a pleasing spectacle / cut did not make the boast to have found / found / argued from utterly false premises / lay opposite / are not kept / but are kept / was unquestionable proof / was thoroughly cleansed / are not everywhere equal / is hollowed out to receive / cut / cut / it occurred

am very sorry / did not think / was not possible without the help of many men to do so / thought / saw / cut / neither saw nor wish to conjecture / is detached / forms rather a species of cavity / feeding / rests / ended / cut / found / secreted in consequence of the slow and distressing death of the animal / detached / shine through like a tree / cut

trust / observed / saw only through a lattice / seen / stating / explaining / observed / captured / spoil with teeth / steal / studying / worried / writing / hire / tear to pieces / commended / to bring home with / saw / to bring home at least the spoils / narrating / feed / never saw / never heard / saw / misinformed / describe / make like the Platonic man / bears resemblance / impresses as being like / feeds / say nothing / moving / it happened / was helpless and unable to get away / should be tamed / can be tamed through stupidity and greediness / it happened

hook / secured / took / entered / held / stood / holding / struck / held in spite of frantic efforts at resistance / dragged / held / wore out by constant blows / rendered thoroughly passive by spears / finished by knives and other weapons / drawn to land / cut while still alive

did not find / think / it happens / breathe differently from fishes / can better swallow / more easily taken / move about / get free by tearing hook out of skin / saw / caught / endeavor to assist / try to upset boat / endeavour to extract the hook from the back of wounded companion with a blow from their tails / several times proved successful / cut / found still waiting / utters no sound / only breathes heavily and seems to sigh when wounded / will not venture to assert how much their eyes and ears are worth / see and hear little / seem to neglect and despise the use of these organs

have written / published in English in London / correspond / says / says / hunting / approach without noise and without speaking / caught in great numbers / eat / called by the inhabitants, in their language / must tell the uses / are put to use / stretch / use in the same way as / use / becomes yellow like May butter / cannot be compared

can be kept / approximates / nearly can be used for / its use is not to be despised / it moves gently, producing / can be kept / lives / prevents / preserving / work even more powerfully / cooked / to distinguish / resembles / can hardly tell the difference / when boiled it soon becomes tender / boiling / swells up like young pork / takes up / does not really refuse / becomes quite like corned beef / did not try to do much / had a great abundance / it moves

Lip Border

Sometimes when I'm reading
I lose concentration and notice
between the whitespace and the letter
a border like the lip
at the border of a wound.
The page is soft and pliable skin,
sometimes wet and swollen.
The letters, still healing.
A redness around them, maybe.

The letter with blood enters, they told us,
as they engraved on us the Law,
and we gave up our watery ways
to become rigid as stones.

We then asked to be photographed
beside a stone effigy of ourselves.
Fluorescent flip-flops on our feet
in place of real emotions

This Wall

It bites into our land like snakes, said the poet, *it cradles*

a circle around the bones of *Rachel,* whose womb

as she watered the flock

was brimming with stones and days and mourning

and who even in death belongs

to the patriarchs – they did after all

work fourteen years to buy her hand in marriage. And so to
    this day

the wall

out of nowhere, absurdly nine metres

tall in fortified cement,

on the wealthside glistens referencing ficticious invaders

on ourside reeks of the blood of martyred children

I place my hand on one of the concrete slabs, warm from the sun which till this day refuses to be Occupied

and yes, there is a wounded dove with a sprig of olive in its beak. Red spray paint over the gap between two slabs drips from the words

Je t'aime Palesti

ne

The Overburden

to Sergio González Rodríguez

We watched as they flayed the earth
muscles pulsating under topsoil
topskin bunched up under the scraping tool

We had loved the mountain's beauty as the creases
around our mother's smile

We called it 'the overburden'
and in full swing unpaired we indexed earnings
invited ourselves to walk the bloodred carpet
up the staircase amidst flashing successes

We said "the surface material
covering the valuable deposit"

Because it is running out, we must steal faster
because we were taught
because the law of money is greater
because

It is winter still and the earth is thawing.
We erect barriers of dry branches like the pagans
the water is dragged here in wheelbarrows

And we allow the torn mountains
to wrap themselves again around the silver

To place the body between the cogs
to dig in the body for the valuable deposit
to open the body
to make a triangular incision in the body

To cross the border of the body
to be the midwife of the body
to pull out with pliers from the body
to pull the braids of the body
to distinguish the body
to feel with the body's fingers
to forget the weight of the body
to structure the body
to flee from the body
to cross the line dividing the body

To hear the sand sing
the lizards scuttle between the rocks
the routes traced by bison across

The body with most traffic
the body enjoying a moment of solitude
the body unknotted
the florid body
the body that frequents night clubs
the broken body
the tamed body
the body found in Lote Bravo
the body that does not demand respect
the body on the edge of the bed, throat half slit
the pitcher body
the body that rises for work when it's still night
the body painted with sheet creases
the body arm of the industry
the cyborg body
the body with hands tied with the laces of her
    own shoes
the body that needs to be accompanied by a
    man
the body in black plastic bags

the body that is the temple of god
the body from whose nipples nourishment flows
the body that does not belong to the body
the colonized body
the body folded between seat and steering wheel
mind body
abaseable body
dishonored body
intoxicated body
brown body
long-haired body
the body found in Lomas de Poleo
the body so filthy it is not a person
the body with sleeves open like fucsias
the body astray
the body dumped alive
the body left unrecognizable
the body lacking sufficient information
the body with no marks of strangulation
the body with the full force of the law
the effaced body
the body that drew circles with the pelvis
the body in search of opportunities
the migrated body
the self-improved body
the rebellious body
the bone remains of a body
the teeth of a body memorized by a mother
the body separated from the soul
the body recognised by its tattoos
the body found in Cerro Bola
the body planted like a message
the body with a voice ignored
the pillaged body
the looted body

As Joshua Whitehead said,
"the best part
about having
no body
is that i cannot be shamed"

That's why we got rid of our body
that's why we took off our body like giftwrap

The body that knew
the body that desired

The body in a dorsal decubitus position

The now deceased woman
moved like a serpent in bed
allegedly

Letters to the Global South

Dear South,

I have learned to come undone
like a scarf whose purl stitch I dropped way back
at the beginning.

I pull my yarn out of the weave
and it multiplies like in a miracle.
I let the line sag, limp and
creased into
neat little ws ws

and learn to redo it all

§

Dear South,

Thank you for sending us your choicest foods X
How much avocado and quinoa salad
must I eat to fit into that dress, do you reckon? X

In exchange, please receive these trade agreements
you never agreed to X
These weapons for small and large-scale kills X
These drones X

Did you know the sky is very grey today? X
But we had the most beautiful chocolate cake X

Let me explain: here X
we sign all our messages with the Saltire X

it's supposed to represent a kiss X
but it looks like a prohibition like a "do not go further", like
   a "death by torture", like X
the message ends in this precise spot X
here X
where the two lines, yours and mine X
lock horns. X

~~Where my upper lip and your lower lip~~
~~meet: a kiss wrapped~~
~~in pain.~~

That's just how we kiss here. X

§

Dear South,

~~The kiss perhaps also recalls an obscure, masculine pain.~~
~~The martyr on the X-shaped cross~~
~~in reality had no name:~~
~~he was nicknamed "andras": ανδρας~~
~~which means simply, "man."~~

~~And it's as if we, too, rootless, have been looking~~
~~for a name this whole time~~

§

Dear South,

I've been looking for traces of you on my Instagram feed.
A corner where the Coca-Cola logo is hand-painted onto the wall
and packs of feral dogs sniff around the bins.

In you I had a ghost dog
who followed me around wherever I went.
It was a yellowish white crossbreed:
an ugly old thing, that never barked or was hungry.
Late at night, his nails peppy on the cobblestone.
His sigh as he slumped beside me after a long trek.

Here, in the North, we've had all our ghosts cleared out
with the bins that didn't adhere to the council's rules
and with that
we forgot about death.

A dangerous way to live. But your ghosts
still wander the city

§

Dear South,

I remember the smell of rotting flesh on hot cement
the grains of saliva on the corner of a just-awake mouth
the air heavy with particles, the greasy air
and the sunset cutting spectacularly through the dust
and how the night sky through till dawn was hot as the lights
    at the fairground.

That night I walked barefoot in the dark like a beggar.
The sewers overflowing, the trash bags piling up into pyramids.

~~The packs of rats and stray dogs~~
~~and ghost stray dogs.~~

I'm on the wealthside of the wall now, but I've always been
on this side
of the wall: even when I walked barefoot I was a tourist.

~~The sleepless guards never asked for my ID or my reasons~~
~~for entering the gated villages where the rich kids slept~~
~~behind bars under placid palm trees~~

§

Dear South,

I was able to buy a plot of land in you
for the price of maybe a dozen paninis in the North.
On the shadowy half, I built a barn.
On the sunny half, I lay down in the field.

We covered your coasts with cement tower blocks, it's true.
Bleached their bones and regimented the windows.
We thought we'd vacation there all the time.
Float supine in azure pools beside the sea.
At restaurants the ruffles of pink chiffon were
anemonies in the salt-crust breeze.
Shiny coins fell into the cups of musicians
from distant lands.
We ate fish, grilled whole, though we
didn't quite know how to deal
with the bones. In the North, we never used to have to
deal with the bones. Someone else did that for us.

I for one never knew you could lift
the whole backbone clean from the meat
pulling the head and tail along with it
in one piece like in a Hannah Barbera cartoon

§

Dear South,

In the mountains, the pits are still open. The bodies are still
being piled in. They have no names, because you know
we are all one. That North and South
we are all, even as we go about our day,
sleeping in a pile,
in a grave up in the sierra. It rains
warmly on us. Our flesh swells. We feed the coyotes, and look up
when the train's howl tears through the heat yonder

§

Dear South,

Because I carried it around with me, in my body,
I never noticed the depths of the sorrow in your face.

Now I pick at the bones of it: your childish silence
your scraped knee and your torn wine-coloured polyester
trousers caked in dust, your foot kicking at the gravel.

~~There was always so much gravel around,~~
~~wasn't there?~~
~~Or was it rubble?~~

§

Dear South,

The tower blocks are lying empty now
their calcareous growth a negative cast
of the flesh that inhabited them.

~~What hermit crabs will use them as a~~
~~scavenged shell? Where do they hail from?~~

§

Dear South,

I'm sorry to hear you lost
everything.

That your family home is now
a pile of stones.

And still you stand at the doorstep
of this pile of stones

and cheerily say *chai, chai!*
inviting me in for tea

On Love and Dying Languages

In our broken mother tongues
in our English plain
in our rented room
in our foreign country
with our migrant friends
little by little we built
a vocabulary known only to us.

For example:

kamilo, derived from my word for walking
and your word for camel
meant 'the path travelled through the desert'

pardo, was 'the spots of light
burned into our eyes after staring at the sun',
also 'dusk', or 'a ginger cat'

but kamilopardo: 'cute' or, 'let's make babies'

thalassa, from your word for the sea
and my word for cutting down trees
was used to mean 'it aches at the pit
of my stomach',
or 'I understand',
or 'we love it because it is unattainable,
like the end of the rainbow,
or the unique phenomenon
of a distance,
however close it may be'.

We developed our own syntax.
The present continuous was always being lost.
Articles were obviated.
Dreams were something we saw, rather than had.
There was no indirect object.
The future was an act of purity of will. For example:

> *shlixá*, the word for 'excuse me',
> was used to mean 'do you maybe have a cigarette?'
> the 'maybe' being an important marker of politeness
> like when the Israeli government phones you to say
> your house will be demolished in 10 minutes
> instead of catching you unawares.

There were also things that were never to be mentioned:

 the word *bitterness*
or the word *sorry* when criticised

§

One day I had to go. I was called
to work, to serve in the army, or to tend to my grandfather's death.
You had to stay. Finish your book, or school,
make turmeric tea for your mother.

At the other side of the ocean, I let the sun
pierce my eyes with its needles,
instructing each muscle in my face
not to contract.

I thought of a silk thread, joining my tear duct to yours.
I called the thread *pardo*, and sang songs at my grandfather's
    deathbed.
'This is what I have come *para*,' I said to myself.

Para being a new preposition
which meant both 'from' and 'to'
in terms of origin and destination.
It had the added advantage that, to you,
the word *para* meant both 'alongside', and 'beyond',
the way people stick together
through thick and thin.

I fell asleep every night repeating the word *thalassa*
in every outbreath, like a wave crashing against the cliff
where your house was perched.
I thought this was helping you sleep.

You wrote me a letter saying
you hadn't slept a wink for months.
That the waves heightened your senses

§

Before we got separated,
we used to play a game
to while away the miles
as they rolled under our feet:

Exoume spiti stin Tourkía? Do we have a house in Turkey?
Nai, exoume. Do we? Where?
Stin Eskişehir, near the central mosque.
Oh yes, that's right. That's where we held a massive feast
after Ramadan.
Kai exoume spiti stin Aboudabi?
Nai, we do.
Oh I forgot about that one. How many bedrooms in that one?
It has five bedrooms, and a swimming pool.
Who's looking after that one for us?
A businessman and his family.

I'm glad he takes such good care of it.
Exoume spiti stin Costa Rica?
Yes, *exoume spiti* in Costa Rica.
Oh, you're right, is that the one that looks like a German villa?
Yes. *Kai exoume spiti stin...* Japan?
Nai, exoume, stin Tokio. It's cute but not enough space.
That's why we don't go there very often.
Kai exoume spiti stin Glaskovi?
Nai, kardia mou. Remember? It's that big mansion in Hyndland
that looks like a castle. That's where we like to
spend the autumn months.
Kai exoume spiti stin Mumbai?
Yes, that's the one with 27 stories
layered seemingly haphazardly
like bricks of Jenga.
It's alright but it takes too long
to get from one room to another.
I might be dead before I manage
to walk the length of that hallway.
Exoume spiti stin Finlandía?
Yes, that's just a little luxury tree house.
It's good for summer, when the rest of Europe
is blazing like a kiln.
Kai stin Australia?
Yes, a very bohemian colonial house
with a big garden. That's where I beat you at basketball
the other day.
Kai exoume spiti stin México?
Nai, we do and after long journeys
we always fill our bellies
with the most delicious food
Kai stin...

That way, we never felt homeless, even though we were fleeing
all manner of calamities

Lines of Algebra

His sleep was dark.

The city
was swallowing our money
and flashing it at us again
like a coin pusher machine.

I lay awake,
a Tibetan hungry ghost
whispering grains
of sand:

one by
one
falling
from my lips
to his ear.

I watched the storm roll away, the blue
way the skyline
was coming into view.

The house sighed,
out of breath. How hard
it was working
to keep us
in

§

One grain
of sand is still stuck
in my throat. I cough,
cough

for an ablution
like the reflection of water
on the side of the boat.

Make me
what I am
(said the boat to the water)
because I've never
been able
to be it alone.
Because I know nothing
else but the print of your hand
where you struck me
(said the boat to the water).
And why is this of note?
That the water in its ways
knew where the ache was.
Where, medicinally,
to put the kiss.

The more you hurt me (said the boat) the less
it hurts

§

We wake
late and sticky.
The little cough still lodged
in my throat like a crumb or a gruff
repetition of performativity:

"I'm this, I'm this, I'm this."

He offers me water and I barely "mmm"
unsure if this means yes or no.
To him it's a yes.
So I drink

§

Cold water
down the centre
to fold myself in half
and then in half again
lift the pleated flaps
till I'm a math paper
boat.

Splay myself out again,
show the folds.

Must smooth down,
not let the water gather
or slide in straight
lines.

I'm this, cough, I'm this, cough

§

From my throat I pull a red thread,
almost living.

I pull long, long.

Lanky lines
of red algebra are drawn.
This is my maths problem:

one plus one plus one
does not make a marriage, but listen.
His voice is hollow
and wind, like birds' bones

Sweet of the Spoon

The streets of the hungry city
teased me with their sunglobes
singing tales of sweet water
against the blistered blue.

The shade dusted
onto white walls,
an imitation of summer hotels.
Breakfasts not had on balconies.
Even the ghosts had stopped coming.
It seemed the city where your mother lived
hadn't eaten for weeks.

Grey streets piled with orange fruit and I asked why
people didn't eat.

You said they are the bitter kind,
inedible unless cooked into preserves.

Your mother lay mewling on the sofa:
mamá mamita mami, she called
after her own mother, all hospitals closed.

You went in at four-hour intervals
to feed her medicine with a spoon,
never explaining what it was for.
She opened her mouth wholly trusting.

Suffocated by the heat in the house, I
spent my days watching ant trails
at Exarchia square. A toothless anarchist
offered me wine in a carton.

("O for a beaker full of the warm *South!*")
Told me of his friend beaten to death
by the fascists. Of his other friend
succumbed to heroin. Of his other
friend kicked out of engineering school
as the university shrank. Of his
other friend arrested for being gay.
I was too distracted to listen. I knew
he had love packed in a jar
somewhere like a precious marmalade
of Porto. It was called "sweet of the spoon,"
where did he keep it? I rolled
another cigarette, in expectation.

I wanted love fed to me with a spoon:
the bitter packed in sugar glass:
me, like a hungry pup, blindly sapping
gold from the shreds of peel, the tacky
crystal-cut flowers. That's what I wanted.

Your mother didn't know
she was dying.
She drank her medicine like a good girl.
No questions brewing.

I wanted you to reason with her: mother
you are dying. We are sad.
We weep. We thank you. Good-bye.
Was it not her right to know
these were her last days?

Because you wouldn't say –
because she wouldn't ask –
I started making preserves
with dusty oranges I gathered from the street.
My flesh powdery. My peel heavy with metal.
I thought if I wouldn't be fed
I could feed others to a similar effect.

I tried to sing as the sugar boiled away:
tu nombre es un nombre común como las margaritas
but my voice caged. Pack more sugar into it:

We don't put sugar in the bitter
but bitter in the sugar.
It's not the sugar which makes the bitterness tolerable;
it's the bitterness which makes the sugar good to eat.
Gives it depth.

(The mother never re-married.
The memory of the father washed
through her ribcage. The son suckled
her inky breasts, and was dark.

My throat filled with the spolia
of their speak.)

The houses were being demolished.
The people kicked out
to the streets but I still tugged
at your sleeve for the sweet
of the spoon, withheld.

You shrugged me off like your mother's whine,
but whispered in my ear days later:
s'agapó.

Love was a galloping rage agazapado
of needle and sponge.
I cooked more preserves. Carried tubs
of it to Exarchia square.
I wanted to feed the starving anarchists
wholly holy like a saint.

"Where did you get this?" they asked.
"The oranges are going to waste,
piling and rotting on the street.
There is abundance around us
if you know where to look!"

I thought I had learned their
methods, their language.

They said, "You still need money to make fire,
to cook the oranges in sugar for hours. And the sugar,
how much did that cost?"

Becoming

We met up at the station.
You were just out from work, suited, trilby hat.
Long hair tied back, and shades.
At my place, you asked:
do you want to see me? Half-opened
your bag to show me the materials
and I watched you
take away layers
        buckle, knot, button, gold-plated
        cufflinks, the careful fold
showing all your skin to then
cover it
again with other strata
thong
tights
corset
bra
like this, you said
a satiny top, bespangled, miniskirt
lick of liner
eyelash.
The more you added
        heel, earring, feather, blush,
your shoulders turned more candid,
your gestures more delicate,
your ways more sunny and plain,
till you became
completely
you

Skinwater/Waterskin/Skinwater

[*Skinwater*]

Lines cross over each other forming diamonds deformed on the
    surface of the river
like the lines on the fissured desert earth, or your arms

[*Waterskin*]

the drier the skin, the clearer the lines,
more texture. The older we are the more text we are,
more ourselves.

This is beautiful. I tell you
there's no way for you to understand
your beauty.

I tell you this and your face softens all of a sudden
the way a bubble full of water bursts.
Letting fall a fleet of emotion
and lifting up
a smile that makes clouds spin.

Something parts around your mouth
the way a waterfall parts
forming curtains around the stone
and it's as if the word "beauty" has washed something
leaving only the essence

[*Skinwater*]

Chasing rainbows on the S-Bahn
I take a picture of the sunset to send to you but all you get is a blur
and the tacky unicorn sticker from my phone
reflected on the window.
My trajectory undisturbed, like an orbiting planet,
the course of eight rivers and all the Bahns me van llevando
bringing me closer

The Task of the Translator

Hold the concept
as a dear hand
learn its scars, its temperature
the parts hardened by work
the weight with which
it will lead, or be led.

One day: try
words on
one after the other
like rings;

another day: the first
ring chosen
a perfect fit:

how joyfully
the metal glints
for having found
printed on skin
by lack of sun
a band, as if the ring

had been there
all along

The Guitar's Lament

I recently reached the conclusion that I am a guitar.
There were numerous clues that suggested the above, but
          until now
I had lived blind to them.

Firstly there are of course my handsome curves
the resonant hollow in my chest
my stiff arms
the tension of strings that keep me tied
to who knows what hair-raising notes of the past.

To that we must add my ability to align my body
against that of a musician
my fondness for the numbers 5 and 12
my being able to sound only when strummed
my inevitable position as an object
my connection to balconies and bad poets
my repeatability in simple chords
my dusty fretboard
my fixed form
my frustration at not being a hat
or a bird
or a tree
or a violin at least.

Every day I rise early for work
hang from a wall
or a shoulder
or sit on a knee
and repeat the phrases of the dead

phrases that are not mine
lever of the histrionic
ancient shell.

One thought and only one
brings me solace: that endings are mere artifice.
Nothing starts or ends. Not even I
started at my navel or end at my skin

The Christmas Tree

A couple of months ago I had my skin surgically removed and replaced with a network of incandescent light bulbs in four different colours, like a Christmas tree. Each time I breathe in, the lights swell and expand a little, blurring at the edges as if trying to cover the gaps in between. When I breathe out, it's like I'm blowing out a candle, and for a moment I am still in my own darkness. Then I'm on again.

/ Off. // On. /// Off. /// On. // / Off. // On. // ///

My favourite thing is to try and make my lights reach further and further, just to see how far I can go. So I might be sitting in this little room but my skin reaches all the way to Brazil sometimes. It's a strange feeling, my muscles and bones and things all exposed, tingly and warm from the light bulbs. I can't quite tell if it's painful or if it feels good. The breeze is slightly astringent on my organs. I don't like to look down, though. I'm afraid I might make myself feel sick seeing myself open up like that. Or I might be too tempted to prise the gaps wider and contemplate the inner workings of my body. No. What I want to do is send colourful, intermittent lights as far as they will reach. Did you know that the favelas in Brazil are painted in bright colours already? I'd seen them in pictures before but they really are bright beyond description. So taking my Christmas lights there might seem like carrying river stones to the river. But still, that's what I do

My Seven Poet Selves

Nighttime in Valetta. My seven
poet selves clamber down
to gaze over the black waves and the sandstone fortress.
We stand artfully arranged down the descending rocks.

The moon is full of liquid and splitting
at the sides like an over-ripe watermelon.

Suddenly, the Surrealist poet kicks off his flip-flops
exorting the Exotic poet, who doesn't speak any English,
to do the same, tugging her arm towards the water.

"She can't swim!" the rest of us yell, knowing
she comes from the desert, hundreds of miles inland,
and has never seen the sea.

The Goth poet – who has not shown a hint
of emotion all week – freely admits to her maternal side,
but doesn't know how to scold them to safety
without losing her cool.

The Surrealist yells,
"Exactly! She has never been in the sea before!
Do you understand?"

As they both step further down towards the water,
we all guess at the slipperiness of the rocks,
calculating how long
it would take us to run down and jump in after them
at the first sign of drowning.

The Career poet has barely said a word all night, though she did
mumble softly in agreement
at the idea that they should perhaps wait till morning for their
    swim.
She leans falsely relaxed against the railing, wearing
the same amiable smile.

The Lyrical poet marvels at our interconnectedness,
how at one our spirit is with both sea and ancient fort,
at which point the Exotic poet
hangs from a rock to dip one foot in the water.
We all gasp, half fearing for her life
half imagining what it must feel like –
that first contact with the buttery water.
She climbs back to safety, and we cheer for her

but then gasp again
when the Surrealist leaps to his feet and strips off.
"Don't do it! Please!" we yell, but he dives right in.

When we see what a great swimmer he is, we relax,
almost stop paying attention.

I, the Alcoholic poet, take it all in with another sip of beer,
and sigh, welling up:
"I love you guys – my poetry gang."

The Goth poet laughs
imagining a nineties rap cover album
with eight badly dressed poets doing inscrutable hand signs.

At this point, the Language poet, whose books
nobody has ever read, glowers at the Surrealist,
who has now climbed back to safety
and, not yet having properly dressed again,
is delivering a proto-fascist self-improvement tirade
at the Exotic poet, who may or may not be understanding any
    of it,
but probably feels patronised either way:

"Apart from your own fear," says the Surrealist, "you must
    conquer
the fear of the Others. Never let anything
or anyone prevent you from
taking that leap into the void."

"I can't take this anymore," says the Language poet,
whose poetry has tested the patience
of even the most studious scholars.
"I'm going home," he says,
and that's when we split

Fly Ash Slurry Spill

It's midnight in October and the rain is on fire
and I walk through the dappled

                              branches flung
onto medical buildings oranged by Glasgow's
not-yet-LED lamplights

And my voice doesn't touch
the darkened windows or the anatomy
students absent in their

                        theatres

Or my shadow   as I walk with it: her
wet hair flat   on her scalp: her
shoulders   hunched: her
coat the smell of   last winter

We light one word   with the previous like a chain smoker
tight in fingers   up to our lips
blow flick   remains onto remains
fly ash   slurry-spill

(The Brutalist hospital is   bulldozed half-open
and the mint blue tiles   on the wall stand bloodless
and the cross-sectioned rooms   empty now except for
our thoughts lying   neatly tucked in dusty beds
curtainrailed   out of view
where one Friday night   a stabbed man
and the doctors' trainers   squeaked against linoleum
where needles'   plastic wrappers
and vials   were tipped into   labelled bins
with their Antrhopocenal hygiene of   plastic layers

Where a heart was kept alive   outside the body
    (be still, in this icebox, my –)
and a patient held their spent   heart in their hands
its ochre, fatty sinews   before it was safely disposed of)

We don't know yet   about the earthquake in November
where a   town's only hospital
collapsed, all   patients and staff
under

But we know the earthquakes in September that
shook our friends' hearts up to their   uvulas
and how they clawed through bricks and lifted
together
themselves out of the   pool of ghosts

While us here, alive, alive, are alone
our words burning at the coal seams
since 1668
unspoken

Thirteen Ways of Inhabiting a Language

on listening to my friends read Janet Paisley's poems in Scots

Reading Scots on the page, to me,
a non-native of these lands,
is a bit like trying to read an architect's plans:
I can see how it makes sense in theory
but I find it hard to visualise the home
as a three dimensional, living, breathing entity.

The poems walk and talk to me but don't have the same swagger
as when read out loud.

So I ask my friends to read to me
poems as Whatsapp voice messages
that I can play over and over at bedtime.
(So much of friendship, nowadays
takes place in the sphere
of the tiny speaker in my phone.)
My friends guide me into dreamland
with the wind in their vowels
curlin around the els
rappin at the ars.
Their voices grow sweeter
and take on a certain formality
not like the poetry voice from school
but neither like the way they normally speak
as they caress the sacredness of Janet's rhymes.
Katy says, That's not how I talk.
I'm not sure how to pronounce that.
I had too look up certain words.
I'll give it a bash, says Sophie.

I found it hard to make those shapes with my mouth, says Debbie.
All hailing from Glasgow, and a lot more Scottish than I,
they read with a tentativeness that gives me permission
to be playful.

I repeat into the mirror as I listen:
their ars rolling around the muirs
their els liltin and birlin over the water
their double oes where I'm used to bowing down to power
their ees stretching my facebones higher
their aes identical to the ees but wide with an almost-laugh
their liquid ues in the muine-moon
their ies a double positive,
the surest affirmation.

Marie Kondo likes to knock on books
the way you'd knock on a friend's door
to wake them up.
I text my friends and ask them to read to me

 Yin: *tae rest on*

Uno: tae restar el resto.
Rest the rest y descansar.
To forget one's yang and reach
instead for yon
yin pond of stillness:
nae wind to stir things up, nothin movin.
Deeper yet, swimming down
(*the watter in the burn gaes by wi hurley a wrinkle*)
to the darkest parts,
arms out like a sleepwalker's
to reach hasta palpar the wound

all wound up in scar tissue
and threads de historias deshilachadas
frayed tapestries, the stories all
unwoven

Twa: tae be at odds, richt or wrang

In the old joke, being right was just a meringue.
But other days
when the wrong ran and rang louder
rancio de rigoris mortis:
qué afán de estancias tersas
dos al son
de quién tiene la razón
de quién tiene la canción
más desdichada.

One two one two
check check check
yin twa yin twa
check check check
un dos un dos
together
un dos un dos
juntos juntos juntos

There's a word in Italian which I always struggle to translate:
confronto. Sounds so much like confrontation which sounds
so much like anger which sounds so much like a bull charging
against the red. But in Italian, confronto means something
midway between compare and contrast, face to face, forehead
to forehead, thick as thieves, fighting some, yielding some, also

just talking a lot, locking horns or not, head on, coming up against, lots of hand gestures. In context: father and son had a lot of good confronto. Translation: they talked a great deal after dinner. Not in order to find out who was right, but in order to grow. An exchange which may involve some amount of confrontational posturing, quarrelling as an encounter of spot the differences, investigating comfort zones and boundary lines, and Who Are You? asked the caterpillar. But no, really, who *are* you. I'm very interested in *not* projecting my fantasies all over you, said no one ever

Three: wheit awthing comes in

A trinity of needs: angling for the recognition of one who
echoing with need to know its name:
the Other there
the first keek at yon wee inch
Tres tres trés mon trésor.
O sorcières, ô misère, ô haine!
Enter un viento pálido, color espíritu

Fower: squares yon circle

Escuálido círculo a circus of chalk.
Tidy and straighten up those curves.
Equilateral sides and protection,
the way it always used to be.

Reaching back to the past – what is that? Strong and stable? I once befriended a rock and roll band. Their music style and the way they dressed was so seductively retro. Unfortunately, so were their politics. In the worst sense. More than once I heard them heteronomatively lament: Oh why must it be 2019 and not 1975? The days when we could leave our engines running on progress, fossil fuels and hope for the future

Five: kin git the wark done

The Spanish word for work, *trabajo*, is to travail: to toil, labour, laborar, lavoro. A traversing of fields of effort and pain. The word *travelling*, which entered the English language around the 14th century, comes from the same root as *travail*. The semantic development reflects the laboriousness of pilgrimage in the Middle Ages: less tourism and more self-sacrifice, pointless work to appease the gods. The word *travel* replaced the Old English *faran* – going, course, journey – aran andando andariegos andras andrajosos. A word literally travelling to its own demise via the pilgrimage routes.

The Spanish word for travelling, *viajar*, is to via crucis. Via cross the cracked earth, sorrows as our only luggage. Our language faraning far away. Farewell!

Words are such good travellers
they pick up meanings as they go

Sax: tae mak a warld

Going for the long six or the oxling here.
The sound is produced by an oscillating reed
an air column whose resonant quality is changed
by keys with shallow bowls
cupping the sound, cradling it until
it sings the world anew

Seiven: quarters the muine

Words in a book, closed off
hidden from view
pressed like petals
translucent
silently awaiting their turn
to be brought to life again.
Spoken out loud,
the poem is brought back to its homeland:
the body, the voice,
the mouth wanting to wrap itself around the words
like they're apples as we bite off
more than we can chew.

Bones sung up from the glen
or whispered over the moors
birlin ower the watter
or stammered in closes
(the "close" signifies how far from our neighbours
much like in Scandinavia, the architect explained to me)
or melted like an ice cube in someone's drink

softening the edges of the sky

Aicht: ower mickle tae love wi

Muckle amor, mucho love.
I don't muck about.
I always sign off my emails
– even work emails – with eight exes.

Think of an eight laid out on its side
to represent infinity.

I know it's not appropriate. I probably come across
as immature, or deranged, or dim, or even a flirt.
But how else can I translate
this boundless love
which needs no object, subject or verb
or split infinitives, possessive nouns, pronouns
action or reaction.
Love which simply *is*.

Hear: back home, I noticed a strange and unfamiliar warmth
birlin lak licht around the lenguas
and the language from out the corners of strangers' mouths.
Even strangers stravaign extraviados
And I says to myself, what is this?
And efter much thought and reflection
I realised
they
are
simply
happy.

Even without a penny split down the middle.

Love is
the only abundance that's
real

Nine: ower muckle tae blether aboot

Nine of us in our coven:
a rabble of rays.
I bask in that sun

Ten: lang enough furra holiday

The Scots way of listening holds a peculiar kind of warmth, and
I mean that in the way the word has of stretching itself out like
a lazy cat across three whole syllables: wah-rum-mth.

I could curl up in that sound
mind them whaur haime is:
in its tiny moon-harnessed tides
the tidings it brings with it
and sleep there all day.

Boat anchored.

Here's tae belang
where a driech blaw kin dicht aff the stoor o stravaign.

When asked why she decided to stay here the birlin traveller
    responded:
"it's the way people speak"

Eleiven: lost tae yon sun dawdlin ahint the muin

What do you do when the sun forgets to come out
in the longest darkness of winter months?
Bueno I go out into the frosted forest
all things twinkling with ice like tiny eyes with a lust for life
and leaves crunching underfoot
glaciers chippit oot her glens
ahint ahint ahí atrás estás
están
las stars
staunin still

Twall: a streetch fae yule tae Christmas tae stymie pagans

We quietly tally our losses.
Our ancient ways of hearing how
the trees speak

Thirteen: fur witches, blue muins an baxters' add-ons

Oor freedoms are aye boucht dear, said the witch.
Each lunation, muskeg fires that had been smoldering for years
blew the smoke eastward, saturating
the air with oily droplets of just the right size to scatter
red and yellow light
and cry back the licht, cry back the licht
making the sun the auld sol appear lavender or blue in colour.
We called it
the blue dazed days,
and we wandered round rarefied, taking in
every second as if all life on earth
were imminently ceasing.
Each breath a gift,
a baker's dozen

THANKS & ACKNOWLEDGEMENTS

Boundless love and gratitude to my family first and foremost, for being present and supportive always.

For the shelter & tea, bonfires on the beach, sparkful conversations, roadtrips, music, sandpaper, dancing in the kitchen, wild swimming, editorial feedback, late night voice messages, and being a part of what home means to me, thank you Louise McVey, Sven Werner, Sebastian & Carlotta; Sophie Hughes; Natalia Cueto & Jenaro; Laia Jufresa; Raquel González Díaz, Liliana Guerra, Daniela Pérez & Dominic Procopio, Leonor Montes de Oca, Alicia LaMadrid, Karla Salinas, Estela Duarte, Olivia Manzanilla, Marisol Martínez Escobar, Greta Alanís Salinas; Svenja Meyerricks, Álvaro Huertas & my god-daughter Tara; Poppy Kohner, Sara Shaarawi, Mark Hesling, Calum Rodger, Henry Bell, Kate S. MacLeary, Katy Hastie, Heather McLean, Roisin Lyle-Collins; Ula Kinderyte; Simon Shaw, Eva Gnatiuk and Emily Chappell of Las Mitras; Becca Murray, Jane Lloyd and Jack of The Raptors; Mohsen Mekhail Najafian; Zoe Zalavary; Anhelo Escalante; Lucy Greaves, Kari Dickson, Kymm Coveney & fam; Jennifer Lynn Williams; Ceylan Hay; Charlotte Prodger; Adrián Herrera Fuentes; Lulú Barrera; Laura Palazón; Carlos Hobbes Treviño; Nicky Arscott; Rike Bolte; Jer Reid; Kate Tough; Paul Johnston, Graeme Miller & Louise Henderson; Andy Brown, Charlotte Arnhold, Cally Archibald; Giorgos Skretis & Nafsika; Lou Dear, Kelly Bornshlegel & wee Ré, wee Beth, Mel Evans, Tilly Gifford, Leonna O'Neill, Hannah Downie, Aimée Lormand; Kate Shaw, Diarmid Baillie, Liam Hurley, Lucy Barge, Jock Barge, Hannah Buss & fam, Robbie Birrell, Scott; Debbie Armour, Becca Harrison, Sophie Sexon, Alexander; Anja Golob; Katharine Eira Brown, Tez Wrigley & Mark Spivey of Rattle; Diljeet Bhachu; Lawrence Schimel, Michalis Mavrotheris, Dimitra Grigoriou, Hazem Jamjoum, Gerry Loose & Morven, Gerry Cambridge, Christie Williamson, Larry & Ratnadevi, Alexandra Büchler, Elin Haf Gruffydd Jones, Mónica Nepote, Rocío Cerón, Minerva Reynosa, Óscar David López, Gabriela Torres Olivares & Jenny Donovan, Charly Olvera, Jaime Martínez, Valis Ortiz, Elisa Lemus, Joserra Ortiz, Calixto Ramírez; Neil Weston; Mónika Ferencz, Balázs Szőllőssy and everyone at FISZ Tábor;

John Z. Komurki; Ulrich Hansen & fam; Katie Presley; Sage Musick & fam, Robbie Reid, Helena Fuentes & fam, Kata Kakuszi; Martí Sales, Robin Myers, Efrén Ordóñez, Giuseppe Caputo, Yolanda Castaño, Luna Montenegro, María José Bruña, Tomás Sánchez, Antoine Cassar, Adrian Grima and our Maltese pirate boat: Laia López Manrique, Clare Azzopardi, Arjan Hut, Jean-Rémi Gandon, Massimo Barilla, Sjón, Ali Althareb, Teodor Reljić, Caldon Mercieca, Nadja Mifsud, Elizabeth Grech, Leanne Ellul, Claudia Gauci, Jean Paul Borg; David Russon. As artists, activists, parents, doulas, wanderers, educators, gardeners, therapists, bar tenders, bike mechanics, partying experts, thinkers, music geeks, general nonconformists and lovers of excellence, your ideas put into action have inspired me and helped me make sense of the world.

Thanks also to all the writers, translators and organisers I've met at the Stammtisch in Glasgow and workshops and festivals in different countries for the lively discussions and warm camaraderie.

Special thanks to JL Williams, Liz Lochhead, Henry Bell and Calum Roger for their feedback on earlier incarnations of this book.

Some of these poems have been published in *Revista Kokoro*, *The Dark Horse*, and *San Diego Poetry Annual*, and translated into Hungarian, Polish, Latvian, Croatian, Slovak, French, Catalan, Frisian, Maltese, Malay, and German. Thanks to the translators and editors for their immense care.

Parts of this book were completed during a Fellowship for Scottish Artists at Banff Centre; during a residency at 33OC in Toffia, Italy; and during my time as a mentee on the Clydebuilt Verse Apprenticeship Scheme. I'm grateful for these opportunities and indebted to the wonderful people I met there.

In honour of the memory of Luis Alberto Arellano, Alexander Hutchison, Tom Leonard, José Antonio Rodríguez, and Sergio González Rodríguez.

NOTES & QUOTATIONS

p.9 'The Serpent Dialogues': Two footnotes borrow from this poem written by Maria Martins: "Even long after my death/ Long after your death/ I want to torture you./ I want the thought of me/ to coil around your body like a serpent of fire/ without burning you./ I want to see you lost, asphyxiated, wander/ in the murky haze; woven by my desires./ For you, I want long sleepless nights/ filled by the roaring tom-tom of storms/ Far away, invisible, unknown./ Then, I want the nostalgia of my presence to paralyze you." Undated manuscript, quoted in Francis M. Naumann, 'Don't Forget I Come from the Tropics': The Surrealist Sculpture of Maria Martins, 1940-1950, Maria: The Surrealist Sculpture, exh. cat. (New York: Andre Emmerich Gallery, 1998), p.p. 22-23.

p.12 'The Serpent Dialogues': *"I shall imagine myself as having no arms, no legs, no body at all"* is a line from Kurt Brandhorst's translation of Rene Descartes' *Meditations on First Philosophy* (Edinburgh University Press, 2010).

p.41 'Juárez / Ecatepec': the numbers refer to the official count of victims in various massacres in Mexico, historical and recent.

p.47 'Flood prayer' draws heavily from Miguel León Portilla's translations of Náhuatl prayers and incantations.

p.54 All the words in 'Steller's Use of Verbs…' are taken in order from Walter Miller's 1899 English translation of Georg Wilhelm Steller's *De Bestiis Marinis*. The original was published in Latin in 1751.

p.70 'Of Love and Dying Languages': The *"unique phenomenon of a distance, however close it may be"* is from Harry Zohn's translation of Walter Benjamin's *The Work of Art in the Age of Mechanical Reproduction*.

p.80 'Sweet of the Spoon': The lyrics *"tu nombre es un nombre común como las margaritas"* are by Brazilian-Mexican singer songwriter Denise de Kalafe.

Juana Adcock is a poet, translator and performer working in English and Spanish. She was born in Monterrey, Mexico in 1982, and was brought up bilingual. Her Spanish poetry collection, *Manca* (Tierra Adentro, 2014), explores the anatomy of violence in Mexico and was named by *Reforma's* distinguished critic Sergio González Rodríguez as one of the best books published that year.

In 2016 she was named as one of the 'Ten New Voices from Europe' and she has performed at numerous literary festivals internationally. She has translated and co-translated some of the most exciting writers working in the Spanish language today, such as Gabriela Wiener, Diego Enrique Osorno, Julieta Valero, Hubert Matiúwàa and Giuseppe Caputo.

She has lived in Glasgow since 2007, where she also makes music with the bands Las Mitras and The Raptors.

Split is Juana's first collection in English and is the Poetry Book Society's Choice for winter, 2019.